JESSIE REES FOUNDATION
CHARITIES STARTED BY KIDS!
BY MELISSA SHERMAN PEARL AND DAVID A. SHERMAN

Published in the United States of America by Cherry Lake Publishing
Ann Arbor, Michigan
www.cherrylakepublishing.com

Reading Adviser: Marla Conn MS, Ed., Literacy specialist, Read-Ability, Inc.

Photo Credits: Photos used with permission from Jessie Rees, Cover, 1, 9, 11, 13, 15, 17, 19, 21; © HugYou / Shutterstock.com, 5; © science photo / Shutterstock.com, 7

LIBRARY OF CONGRESS CATALOGING-IN-PUBLICATION DATA HAS BEEN FILED AND IS AVAILABLE AT CATALOG.LOC.GOV

Cherry Lake Publishing would like to acknowledge the work of The Partnership for 21st Century Learning. Please visit *www.p21.org* for more information.

Printed in the United States of America
Corporate Graphics

CONTENTS

HOW DO THEY HELP?

SOME CELLS ARE BETTER THAN OTHERS

The human body is made up of more than 30 trillion cells. **Cancer** is a disease that gets in the way of healthy cells. It happens when abnormal cells grow and spread too quickly. Bad cells can take over different parts of the body or grow into **tumors**. Tumors happen when these cells group together in a lump or mass.

Healthy cells can grow and divide quickly as well, but they know when to stop.

Some people might help families that have a sick family member by mowing their lawn or walking their dog. Can you think of other ways you could help? Search online or at the library to find other ideas for helping families in this situation.

5

When cancer is found, it is important to treat the bad cells. Every day, doctors are coming up with new ways to fight cancer. While far more common in older adults, cancer sometimes puts children at risk of life-threatening illnesses.

In March 2011, Jessica (Jessie) Joy Rees, age 11, was diagnosed with a rare **pediatric** brain tumor known as DIPG. Her doctors decided she would first go through **radiation**

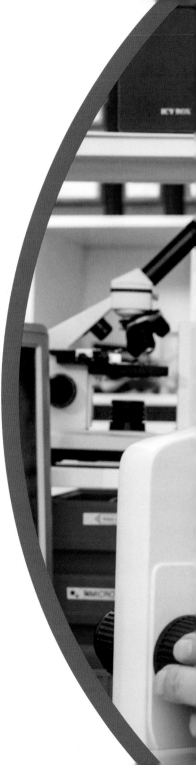

Some tumors have cancer in them, others do not.

LOOK!

In December 2012, Jessie won a Young Wonder award from CNN, presented at the annual *CNN Heroes: An All-Star Tribute*. Take a look online and discover who else has earned this honor.

treatment. This would be followed up by **chemotherapy**.

After her first treatment, Jessie's mind was on the other children she saw at the hospital. The ones who weren't able to leave. Her parents, Erik and Stacey, told her that many of them couldn't go home for a while. Jessie knew she had to help them.

Jessie's plan was to give out goodie bags to cheer up the kids in the hospital. As soon as she got home, she collected brown paper lunch bags, stickers, foam

Jessie started her chemotherapy treatments at Children's Hospital of Orange County in California.

THINK!

Jessie wanted the focus of her charity to be on helping others. What kind of a charity would you start, and what might you call it?

9

letters, and markers. She wrote "Get well soon," "Don't stop believing," and "Hope you're okay" on the bags.

The Rees family checked with the hospital staff on what could be in the bags. The nurses said "yes" to new plush toys and to crayons, activity books, funny socks, and other toys. The family also decided to use large plastic jars instead of bags.

Since Jessie's middle name is Joy and they would be delivering happiness in a jar, they called them JoyJars.

The nurses let the Rees family know not to include used stuffed animals, food, lotions, or sharp objects in the jars.

Why is it better to use a plastic jar than a paper bag? If you guessed that jars are better because they don't fall apart, keep everything germ-free, and look colorful when stuffed, you're right!

CREATING JOY

Jessie created rules for the JoyJars. First rule: no air. The jars had to be super stuffed. Second rule: no cheesy toys. Toys needed to be cool and fun.

Swimmer Jax Shoults, a friend of Jessie's sister, Shaya, posted "Never ever give up," to Jessie's Facebook page. She loved this so much she made it her **mantra**. She shortened it to NEGU (pronounced knee-goo).

"No cheesy toys" didn't mean the toys had to be expensive. They just had to be something a kid would want to play with.

MAKE A GUESS!

Why do you think the nurses insisted that all plush toys be new? Hint: Think about the germs a stuffed animal might pick up and the reason the children are in the hospital.

13

One tough thing about cancer treatment is that patients usually feel worse before getting better. Jessie didn't feel well on the first JoyJar distribution day, so she let the nurses hand them out.

Jessie did watch from a distance as a little boy opened his. When she saw his huge smile, she knew that what she was doing was important.

Friends threw fund-raisers to help her and her family. But the only people she wanted to help were the kids.

As radiation and chemotherapy kill the bad cells, the body works hard to keep up. Many patients who get these medicines feel very sick.

Jessie refused to use cheesy toys, but she loved to include rubber duckies in her JoyJars. What kind of toys do you think would make a JoyJar special?

15

Every dollar raised went back into making the jars. Her goal was to share her NEGU attitude and make sure every kid fighting cancer—about 50,000 in the United States at any given time—received a JoyJar.

The Jessie Rees Foundation started with Jessie's passion to bring joy to sick children.

Because some kids going through chemotherapy end up losing their hair, many JoyJars include beanies. Look online or at your local library to learn how to knit beanies. Maybe you and your friends can make some beanies for kids who need them.

17

JOYJARS® AND NEGU® GO NATIONAL

Erik Rees serves as full-time chief executive officer of the Jessie Rees Foundation. Stacey Rees is the chief operating officer. Together, they work hard to fulfill the selfless mission of kindness that their daughter didn't get to finish in her 12 years of life.

The foundation offers programs that are meant to give "fun doses of hope, joy, and love" to cancer patients and their

Erik Rees was a pastor for 16 years before helping to run the Jessie Rees Foundation. He feels both roles help bring hope to those who need it.

The Jessie Rees Foundation has a mobile Joy Factory that brings everything to companies so their employees can stuff jars together. Have any of your adult family members helped out the community while at work?

families. By the end of 2016, the foundation had reached more than 150,000 children in all 50 states and in 30 countries.

Every year in the United States, about 15,000 kids age 19 and under are diagnosed with some form of cancer. They and their families deserve some happiness, warmth, and kindness. Jessie's family and the devoted people at the foundation, along with over 9,000 volunteers a year, make that happen.

The foundation now also creates sport adventures for kids to meet their favorite players.

CREATE!

Make your very own JoyJar-style creation and find a hospital where you can donate it. Remember, stuff it as full as you can—and no cheesy toys!

21

GLOSSARY

cancer (KAN-sur) the growth of abnormal cells that spread very fast and destroy healthy organs and tissues

chemotherapy (kee-moh-THER-uh-pee) a treatment using medicines and chemicals to kill cancer cells

mantra (MAN-truh) a word or expression that is repeated over and over

pediatric (pee-dee-AT-rik) having to do with the branch of medicine dealing with children

radiation (ray-dee-AY-shuhn) a therapy using intense beams of energy to kill cancer cells and shrink tumors

tumors (TOO-murz) abnormal cells that group together to form a mass or lump

FIND OUT MORE

WEB SITES

www.acco.org
The American Childhood Cancer Organization is the largest national grassroots organization standing at the forefront of the battle against childhood cancer.

http://kidshealth.org/en/kids/cancer.html
Get information about cancer for kids that's free of "doctor-speak."

www.loomahat.com/how-to-loom-knit-a-hat
Watch a tutorial on how to loom a hat.

http://negu.org
Learn more about the Jessie Rees Foundation and what it does.

INDEX

ABOUT THE AUTHORS

David Sherman and Melissa Sherman Pearl are cousins who understand and appreciate that you don't have to be an adult to make a difference.